Little Steps to Millions

A comprehensive guide to building outstanding wealth.

by

Bill P. Beck

TABLE OF CONTENTS

Introduction

Building a $1 million net worth may seem impossible at first, but it is more doable than you might imagine. It's undeniable that everyone has an intense desire to get wealthy! If I told you that there are strategic approaches that can make you a millionaire, you might think I'm crazy. You will have to give up certain things to accomplish this goal, but the sense of financial security is invaluable. If you're serious about becoming a billionaire, it's time to start completing some big measures. Create a well-thought-out plan by incorporating any or all of these easy lifestyle changes set out to make your first $1 million. This content does not discuss any quick fixes for financial success. Nonetheless, you will benefit from particular intelligent guidance that will enable you to increase your savings and maximize the value of your money. You will gain more knowledge about this topic. Going from having little money to becoming wealthy could serve as an example for others using the same basic strategy (spending less than you make, investing the excess, and avoiding debt).

Chapter 1

The Psychology of money

When it comes to money, nobody is completely logical. Even though we think it would be ideal for us, we don't make and stick to a budget or set aside money every payday. We put off creating a financial plan even though we know it's necessary; for some reason, it never happens. We either spend too little out of guilt or too much out of carelessness or excitement. Our financial habits frequently bring us embarrassment.

It is worthwhile to consider your connection with money as being complex. Your money and your personal finances generally are not static; rather, they are a complicated web of opportunities, problems, and data points that you engage with, think about, and feel strongly about. Your financial condition is impacted by the financial decisions you make, and these decisions have an impact on your emotions and subsequent actions.

Also, the relationship changes throughout the course of a lifetime.

The following three points summarize the psychology of our individual connections with money:

• Emotion plays a significant role.

  • Anxiety and avoidance create a vicious cycle.

  • Psychologically, you can't totally leave your family and your past.

Money and feelings

When it comes to money, fear, guilt, humiliation, and jealousy are the most significant feelings. It will take some work to become conscious of the feelings that are particularly connected to money since, in the absence of awareness, these feelings will usually take precedence over reason and dictate how you behave.

What is there to be concerned about? As different as there are unique stories are the possibilities. However, common worries include the worry of running out of things, the fear of appearing foolish, the fear of arousing jealousy, and the fear of being found out or embarrassed.

Shame and guilt are not the same thing.

Shame is the emotion that arises when you let yourself down or fail to live up to your own sense of what's right, whereas guilt is the feeling that you get when you realize that you have negatively impacted someone else.

You may feel bad if you have more than your friends if you haven't given much to charity, or if money has come to you too readily.

One of the most prevalent and potent feelings connected to money and personal economics is shame. It is a major factor in why people refrain from acting appropriately. It makes sense to desire to keep yourself hidden when it comes to something you feel guilty about.

Here are just a few examples of the various forms of embarrassing emotions associated with money:

• I haven't saved enough money; • I haven't thought about money; • I haven't done the things I should have done with money (including setting up a safety net, making retirement plans, and wise budgeting).

• I'm pretty clueless about all of this. • I spend too much.

• I buy goods when I'm sad.

Avoidance and shame combine to form a vicious cycle.

The default reaction when you're feeling ashamed is to turn away from whatever is causing you discomfort. The act of avoiding itself causes further shame and avoidance. The next thing you know, your taxes are past due, and you haven't seen a financial advisor after deciding to finally schedule an appointment six years ago. Individuals who put off taking care of their financial obligations frequently call themselves procrastinators and believe they are simply indolent or lack discipline. That is not helpful and is derogatory and judgmental. What we commonly refer to as procrastination is actually the result of psychological avoidance dynamics. When faced with unpleasant or anxious situations, our brains are programmed to use a variety of avoidance techniques.

The problematic part is that avoidance reduces anxiety in the very short term. You are more likely to repeat it in the same situation since it is effective.

Here's how it unfolds. You're considering sitting down to examine your financial status in detail and coming up with a workable plan. However, the mere thought of it causes your anxiety to increase because you fear you won't be able to accept the fact , for example, you don't have enough money saved for your children's school.

Avoidance is a result of that anxiousness. You put off doing it and find something else to do. Your anxiety level instantly decreases at that point, rewarding you for your avoidance. You keep going through this loop. However, every sudden decrease in anxiety doesn't effectively return you to your prior baseline of suffering. Additionally, as time goes on, your general anxiety level rises.

Contrast this pattern with confronting the unpleasant chore. Your anxiousness spikes for a little while as you accept the reality. But if you stick with it, your total worry will gradually go down. To reap the benefits of the long-term reduction in worry, you must put up with that brief spike in discomfort. The lesson learned in the end is that reality is always on your side.

Envy, greed, over-excitement, and the social psychology phenomenon known as "jumping on the bandwagon" are other emotions that are influenced by money. Certain points are more pertinent in the context of professional investment than they are in personal finance.

Mental well-being and mental disorders

Alcohol use disorder, major depression, bipolar disorder, or ADHD/ADD are the mental health conditions that one in three Americans are likely to encounter at some point in their lives. Every one of these ailments has the potential to significantly impact personal finances.

Overindulgence in alcohol or other drugs results in bad decision-making, financial neglect, job risk, and secrecy.

Depression can result in employment incapacity or even a stalling of careers.

People who are depressed typically lack the energy and sense of purpose to handle their financial obligations.

Bipolar disorder is very challenging. According to current prevalence estimates, this genetically driven illness affects 2.4% of the population. There might be a large number of people with sub-threshold or extremely mild forms who never receive a diagnosis.

Individuals whose bipolar disorder genes express themselves mildly may go through barely perceptible "hypomanic" phases during which they have enhanced energy, lowered inhibitions, exciting plans, are easily overstimulated, and spend more money. In these mental states, many successful and creative people do exceptionally well. However, it's best to steer clear of Costco visits lest you return home with five pineapples, a lifetime supply of ibuprofen, and a brand-new television and treadmill.

Most of the time, adults with Attention Deficit Disorder (ADD or ADHD) are misinterpreted. Its name is misleading. They frequently possess the capacity to pay close attention, as opposed to having an attention deficiency. But only for projects that truly pique their interest. They are able to filter out boring or uninteresting content.

It's easy to miss small details and monotonous chores (think piled-high bills and unread mail). Delegating day-to-day money management is frequently the best option for these people. However, they might excel at large-scale planning.

Childhood and family influences never go away.

Every family has a unique financial psychology. What can be discussed includes who should be in charge, which gender is responsible for what financial duties, and whether or not money is significant.

There are also invariably tales of money playing a role in a family's identity. Perhaps a grandfather who was a serial entrepreneur lost the family fortune, which led to an overabundance of conservatism in the following generations. Or it was perceived that a bright parent had been defrauded of her rightful place in the world.

It's possible that you have felt subtly pressured to make amends for the wrongs committed or endured by earlier generations. Or perhaps there will be an internal push to challenge the family's financial mindset. You could feel compelled to put the needs of the rest of the family above your own financial demands if you're the first in your family to achieve.

How to control your feelings toward money

Not all emotion is negative. It reveals your passions and what is truly important to you. It gives you a sense of life.

Nor is anxiety entirely negative. Anxiety that is mild to severe might be motivating. Use them to confront the things you need to face; you'll feel better after you've done so.

The key is self-awareness. Our emotional environment is largely unconscious. However, if you know what to look for and have a template for the kinds of feelings and family histories that can affect your particular relationship with money, it's not that difficult to access.

Why is it so crucial to comprehend the psychology of money?

We frequently are unaware of the psychological effects that money has on us. However, every single financial behavior we have is influenced by our finances.

Therefore, it is beneficial to understand our feelings regarding money if we hope to make significant behavioral adjustments to our finances or find peace in our connection with it (yes, you do have a relationship with it).

And don't worry—a Ph.D. is not necessary to comprehend this intricate link.

With this column, I hope to help you understand more about your personal psychology as it relates to financial decisions by dissecting the literature and evidence-based research on the psychology of money into easily understood and thought-provoking lessons.

Why it's important to comprehend how money affects people's behavior?

Financial advisors and popular financial advice frequently assert that, with the right support or knowledge, individuals can attain financial wellness or genuinely alter their financial behavior. This presupposes that given access to the most accurate information, all people would act in their own best interests and those of their families as well as other people when it came to money.

If you're anything like me, though, "knowing" isn't always the same as "doing."

You get what I mean? Not "knowing better" equals "doing better."

We can read and educate ourselves on money indefinitely, but as long as we don't change the way we feel, think, and act with it, money will always be the main source of stress in our lives.

Let's talk about financial psychology.

The scientific study of why people manage their money in certain ways is called financial psychology or the psychology of money. Examining how people's financial decisions are influenced by cognitive, social, cultural, and emotional aspects is a broad field of study. Financial psychology, to put it simply, ignores the numbers and is primarily concerned with the human aspect of money.

Do you ever wonder, for instance, why you just can't manage to break a certain annoying financial habit?

Or why do some people hoard money while others spend extravagantly? It can't be a simple case of ignorance. What is causing such urges and decisions?

The majority of the time, the answers are found in our own unique perspectives and attitudes regarding saving and spending.

The unconscious attitudes we have about money, which have been shaped by social, emotional, and cultural influences, frequently dictate how we behave with it.

Knowing your own money psychology is a fantastic place to start if you want to modify your financial habits in a significant way. It's a long-term solution, but it's not an instant one.

"Your life will be guided by your unconscious, which you will refer to as fate until you bring it to consciousness."

Even if we are not consciously aware of them, a variety of behavioral characteristics can have an impact on our financial lives. Here are a few instances:

•"I will show you that I am correct; I know it!"

Confirmation bias is the term for what happens when we search for information that confirms our preconceived notions while disregarding evidence to the contrary. This could obstruct our advancement and lead to self-fulfilling prophecies.

Avoiding confirmation bias primarily requires making balanced, reasoned decisions and actively seeking out information and opinions that challenge our assumptions.

• Loss aversion: This theory holds that people are more driven to keep something than to get something equally valuable. This may cause one to make bad financial judgments, such as clinging to failed investments rather than acknowledging their loss.

It's critical to recognize loss aversion and base decisions on reason and logic in order to make more logical financial decisions.

• Overconfidence bias: This refers to the propensity to overestimate our degree of control and ability in a certain circumstance.

This may cause us to act overconfidently and invest in risky assets like crypto currencies, then hold other people accountable for any mistakes we make.

For instance, a lot of people might have been unduly optimistic about their capacity to execute profitable trades during the 2020 crypto currency boom, only to be let down when the market subsequently corrected.

Making bad financial judgments can result from an overconfidence bias. Recognize this propensity and make an effort to make unbiased, knowledgeable decisions.

How can you benefit from financial psychology?

The goal of financial psychology, counseling, and therapy is to provide an environment for reflection. In turn, that practice develops the self-awareness required to identify the degree to which our ideas, feelings, and behaviors are in harmony or discord. This is essential, particularly in a society that encourages quick thinking.

It enables us to break through the psychological barriers that prevent us from changing our behavior and bring about meaningful transformation.

Why money management is not ingrained in human nature

Now, here's the thing: We weren't designed to manage or save money. As a matter of fact, our default behavior is to spend money. Yes, we may attribute our societal anxiety around finances to our genetic makeup. Because they "saved" food, your ancestors would have been expelled from the tribe.

There was nothing set aside for a rainy day and no discussions about leaving something for the following year or the next twenty years. The capacity to live in the moment and not worry about the future allowed our predecessors to survive and pass on their genes.

This kind of thinking, nevertheless, can lead to issues in the current world, where financial security depends on planning for the future. Our innate psychological characteristics, which were formerly necessary for survival, can today be detrimental to our financial well-being if we don't actively control them.

It's critical to recognize these automatic behaviors and make an effort to control them in order to lessen stress related to money.

In order to raise awareness of the reasons behind our thoughts, feelings, and actions around money, it is imperative that we change the way we think about it and embrace our own money psychology.

How people may alter the impact that money has on them

The best spot to begin? As you examine your own financial psychology, you'll discover that the majority of your financial regrets will make sense.

Consider the views you now have toward money. You will be prompted to consider your unconscious money beliefs by the following questions.

Putting everything into practice:

Take five to ten minutes to consider the following questions:

• In your mind, what does money mean?

• How do you choose what purchases to make with your money?

• How do you feel about money?

• What is your attitude toward money?

Create a giant oval egg on a blank piece of paper, then create one image within the egg for each of the following questions to get the most out of this task.

After looking at each image, write one word that best expresses your feelings.

Next, review your entire article and reflect on the lesson of the money story: "The lesson of the money story in this image is..."

Four Ways Your Money Is Affected by Psychology

I adore studying financial inclinations and the role money plays in a person's life.

Everyone is unique, as I've previously stated, and none of these inclinations are good or bad.

You're just wired that way by nature. I want you to recognize the following four aspects of your financial mindset:

1. Disposal vs. Reserve

Determining whether one is a spender or a saver is generally not too difficult for most people. When it comes to money, spenders see a plethora of imaginative options. I completely relate to this!

Every time I have extra money, it quickly disappears from my pocket because I want to spend it.

A saver, on the other hand, naturally prefers to avoid making purchases with their money. Their sense of relief from having money stashed away is palpable. Savers are willing to wait to make a buy and are patient. Excessive spending poses a risk to both savers and spenders.

You will go bankrupt as a spender if you spend everything you earn. And savers, you will be missing out on a lot of enjoyable activities that enhance your life if you decide to save everything you earn.

When we stop to think about it, this is rather obvious, but the important thing is to consider it.

2. Free Spirit vs. Nerd

Are you familiar with the two categories of budgeters? Math nerds love to crunch numbers. They look forward to setting up their financial plan. Strangers. (Just kidding!) Seeing where their money is going each month and coming up with new ideas to make it function even better makes them feel good. They adore how everything is organized and in its proper spot.

Spirits of freedom are... Well, the celebration is here! We can enjoy life more because we are not overly preoccupied with the minutiae.

The categories for amusement and shopping are essentially your love language, but if you're a free spirit, the very mention of the word budget may make you break out in hives.

Living life to the fullest is what free spirits enjoy!

Nerds require free spirits to provide some entertainment value to the budget for non-essential expenses like birthday celebrations, trips, and late evenings.

The geeks are necessary to assist Free Spirits in creating a reasonable budget. Winston, my spouse, is a nerd, but I adore his keen sense of detail and his awareness of current events.

Before you believe that those who enjoy spending money are free spirits and those who are more prone to save money are geeks, think again. In reality, my dad is a nerd-spender. He enjoys spending money, but he also enjoys monitoring his expenditure.

3. Status versus Safety

Which drives your financial motivation—status or safety? You might need to go through some serious introspection for this one. Think about what drives you to save or spend money, and be honest with yourself. Making the psychology of money work for you depends on this article.

Safety-conscious people crave the security that money can provide.

People desire assurance that they can survive unexpected financial hardships, job loss, or even a medical calamity. Being a safe person means that you have to be careful not to live in dread.

Fear can prevent you from investing for retirement, donating liberally, or even buying new shoes when your daily pair is worn out and needs to be replaced.
For those for whom money is a measure of success, then it is a status symbol. The kind of house they reside in, the activities they participate in, and their capacity to take that ideal vacation are all influenced by their financial situation.

4. Your Upbringing and Family

Your attitude toward money was undoubtedly shaped from an early age by the way you heard your parents talk about it or not talk about it. Though it's important to be aware of, this won't define your money perspective on its own.

Here's an illustration of how financial disputes as an adult might result from past experiences:

Do you become upset and even argue with your partner when they buy, say, brown, organic, cage-free eggs? He objects, saying, "It's just $2 more than the gross white ones.

" You counter, "That's $2 that could go toward something else."

Have you ever wondered why you get so worked up about organic eggs? Is it because you remember growing up your family's shopping budget was a source of stress? Or perhaps your parents scoffed at hippie-dippie, farm-to-table groceries? Perhaps you're a saver-safety person since you didn't have much growing up and, understandably, feel uneasy about spending extra on anything.

I'm not familiar with your history. Perhaps there's something else going on in your life besides a dozen eggs that's making money tense. Here's where self-awareness can result in healing, transformation, and unprecedented growth.

Chapter 2

Easy Steps to Become a Multimillionaire

Ten Easy Steps to Reach Millionaire Status in Five Years or Less

It doesn't matter if you're just starting out or have a large income right now in terms of your financial status.

Whatever their income level, the majority of individuals are just getting by. Spending increases with an individual's income.

Not many people know how to consistently raise their income, standard of living, and happiness all at once.

Establish Objectives

You have to be good at goal setting if you want to become a millionaire. You can ensure your financial future by learning how to set realistic goals for your own money. When it comes to setting financial goals, the same fundamental concepts apply that are important for any goal-making process.

I advise establishing long-term objectives first, then dividing them into smaller, more manageable objectives. Of course, "becoming a millionaire" is your main long-term objective. However, there will be numerous further phases in the process.

Decide on benchmarks, such as reaching a $100,000 or $500,000 net worth. Next, divide those mile markers into even more manageable targets that will ultimately assist you in reaching your final objective.

Make sure the timetable for these objectives makes sense, given your existing sources of income, savings, and financial circumstances.

Although you want to push yourself, you don't want to allow obstacles to stand in your way.

I also advise scheduling regular "time-outs" to think about your objectives and the challenges standing in your way. Ideas that can save you hours, days, and even years of labor will frequently come to you during these moments of calm.

Get Investing

One of the most common ways to become a billionaire is by investing, and with good reason—if done correctly, it may bring in a sizable fortune.

It's important to get into investing early. Benefit from compound interest, which allows you to earn interest on both your saved money and new money.

Retirement accounts are one avenue via which you might invest money.

The stock market, bonds, mutual funds, and even real estate are further alternatives. Speak with a financial expert for assistance if you're not sure where to begin or what's best for you.

Make Use Of A Magic Wand

It's not true that you can wave a magic wand and make millions of dollars overnight. If it was that simple, everyone would follow through. However, you can envision your future achievement by employing what I like to refer to as the "magic wand technique."

Assume you can wave a magic wand over your present predicament or issue. By using this magic wand, all of the barriers that were preventing you from reaching your financial objectives are gone.

If your objective is to establish a profitable company in a specific industry, attempt to look three to five years ahead and picture yourself accomplishing it.

How might it appear? What size would it be? With whom would you be collaborating? What sort of standing would you have in the industry? What would be the sales and profitability level for you? In what manner would you manage this company?

So consider what you could do today to turn this desire of yours for the future into a reality.

Try seeing yourself as a millionaire by using techniques such as these. This will contribute to the development of the millionaire mindset that we previously discussed.Recall that you are the majority of what you think about.

Live Below Your Financial Capacity

Living below your means is making monthly expenses lower than your income. For example, you may make $8,000 a month, but your housing costs and other essential obligations only come to $6,000.

You will then have $2,000 per month to invest or save. You may even lower that number with a little effort to reduce wasteful spending.

Living below your means is a useful and successful way to accumulate wealth and save money. Perhaps you might ask your employer for a raise. However, instead of squandering the excess portion of your earnings on frivolous items, save or invest it to further your aspiration of becoming a billionaire.

Effective budgeting and goal-setting are crucial tools for anyone who is new to living below their means.

Another option would be to downsize into a smaller house or add another source of income.

Consider Yourself A Millionaire

This page contains various strategies that deal with your mind and thoughts: This is a crucial step on your path to becoming a multimillionaire.

Millionaires who made their own way have a common trait. Most of the time, they are prone to thinking in terms of financial independence. Their attention is on reaching their financial objectives, and they consider it frequently. Discipline follows naturally from this perspective. When necessary, self-made billionaires rearrange their financial affairs to make sure they accomplish their objectives. Achieving financial success is not a coincidence.

It requires a highly thoughtful design. It requires millionaire-level thinking.

Engage in "Mind-Storming."

"Mind-storming," sometimes known as the "20-idea method," is arguably the most effective technique for fostering creative thought.

Using this concept, a lot of people—including myself—have gotten wealthy. You might be able to achieve financial independence with just this strategy.

It's easy. Take any issue or objective you have and put it in the form of a question at the top of a piece of paper. You would write, "How can I double my income over the next 12 months?" for example, let's say your goal is to increase your income by double in the upcoming year.

Next, set a goal for yourself to write at least 20 responses to that query. You are required to provide at least 20 answers, but you are free to write more than 20. Just get something down on the page; they don't all have to be flawless.

If you're feeling stuck over how to get more money or improve your financial future, brainstorming is a great approach to keep going.

Conserve Cash

There are two secrets to saving money that will make you a billionaire sooner rather than later. The first is to start early. The second is to put money aside for retirement.

From the time you started working at the young age of 20 until you retired at age 65, imagine that you were able to save $100 per month. You put that $100 a month into a mutual fund that gave you an average annual return of 10%. By the time you retire, your net worth will be about $1,118,000 at this pace.

It's likely that your consistent discipline to save money, no matter how old you get, will have such a positive impact on your personality and character that you'll wind up making much more than 10% annually.

But don't be disappointed if you're further along in life and haven't started saving yet. The present is the ideal moment to start saving and investing for the future.

Eliminate Debt

Pay off your debt as quickly as you can, if you have any so that you can devote all of your attention to your goal of becoming a millionaire. You have a variety of options when it comes to debt repayment.

Among them are:

• The method of avalanches. Pay off your highest-priced loan first. After it is fully paid, proceed to pay off the other debts, arranging them in the highest-cost order.

• The method of snowballs. With your smallest balance, start first. Work your way up to the next smallest balance after paying this one. Continue until you have paid off all of your bills.

• Make multiple payments on your credit card bills each month. You can make sure you don't overlook anything by doing this.

• Pay more than the minimum amount due each month to pay off debt sooner.

• Try to shorten the term of your loan by refinancing your debt. But be advised that doing so can result in higher monthly costs.

• Combine several debts into a single, lower-interest loan by consolidating them.

Lastly, it should go without saying that you should avoid taking on new debt once you have paid off your current debt. Budget wisely and live below your means. Make sure to settle the balance in full each time you use a credit card.

Choose the Correct Path

Most people experience a financial crossroads at some point.

There is one path that goes toward earning, saving, and building wealth.

The alternative results in income, expenditure, and debt accumulation.

Which path will eventually lead to millionaire status is obvious. However, the second route frequently appears to be enjoyable.

Refrain from giving in to temptation! The second route is considerably simpler. However, it won't assist you in achieving your aim. The good news is that you can change course and take the appropriate path at any moment. Just where you're heading matters; where you're coming from is irrelevant.

Every self-made millionaire makes the initial move and accepts accountability for their financial situation. You'll have to follow suit if you wish to become a millionaire.

Maintain Your Discipline

Adhere to the process, and don't give up. A millionaire won't materialize in an instant.

The most crucial thing is to maintain discipline as you pay off high-interest debt, fund your retirement account, and establish a passive income stream.

Sometimes, the key to developing greater discipline is to recognize bad habits and replace them with healthier ones. Perhaps you're attempting to launch a business to make more money, but you enjoy wasting your weekends having fun with pals.

Introduce novel habits on Saturdays and Sundays, such as setting aside time in your schedule to focus on your product. Maintaining these new routines will help you become more disciplined as you pursue your billionaire dreams.

It's not necessary to stop at a million dollars once you understand how to set financial objectives and maintain the discipline necessary to reach them. You'll also be able to make your second and third million.

It's really difficult to reach the first million. However, the second million is all but certain. You should be pleased to hear that.

You will never lose it once you develop into the kind of person who can become a millionaire.

Chapter 3

Common Obstacles To Becoming A Millionaire And How To Break Through Them

I never think I'm worthy of anything. This is the largest challenge for me. I find it hard to believe that someone likes me. I find it difficult to receive money from those who wish to offer it to me.

But wait a moment. Let's discuss the primary challenges to being a multimillionaire.

1) A JOB

And how much will you be paid if you have a job?

For the moment, we'll set aside the average pay because being above average is a prerequisite for becoming a millionaire.

Assume you earn $500,000 annually. Few jobs that pay more than that come to mind.

About half is spent on taxes.

That comes to $250,000 annually. And it's likely that you don't live in the most affordable area of town if your annual income is $500,000.

It is likely that you are paying a mortgage or rent payment of above $100,000. You now make $150,000 annually.

Earning $500,000 annually to maintain a family and children takes time. That is not inexpensive. For example, in Manhattan, you are spending $5,000 per month in the best-case scenario (assuming your children are not attending private school).

You will now need to save $90,000 annually. Including a vacation, unforeseen medical costs, and special expenses, your annual income is likely reduced to $60,000. I'm going to assume everything about you.

On investments, I don't factor in interest. The market rises and falls during the course of a year. The majority of people experienced investment losses. Thus, to acquire about $1,000,000, you need to save money for 16 years while working at the same job.

That is not going to occur. Tomorrow, you might lose your job.

In comparison to inflation, salaries are declining. Dependency on one source of income makes life difficult.

2) HOUSE

Suppose you are instructed to accomplish the following:

Take all of your funds, multiply them by 400%, and invest them in a single venture.

Is there a dividend you receive on that investment? No, the opposite. Annual maintenance and property tax payments are required, and they both increase at random.

Are you able to withdraw your investment? Not really. It's challenging. And it's not possible when you really need the money.

That's the worst possible investment, you would argue.

Greetings from your house.

But isn't renting essentially pouring money down the drain?

No.

As opposed to investing all of your funds in a home. Set aside a small portion of your monthly budget for rent and utilize the remainder to research ways to create other revenue streams or, even better, your own company.

You will be destroyed by a home at the worst possible time.

3) INEXTENSIVE CREATIVITY

You are back with the people if you are without ideas. Not everyone will become a millionaire.

The concept of muscle requires ongoing workouts. Your body will alert you if you skip a few days of exercise: your muscles are atrophying. To be able to walk again, you will require physical treatment if you stay in bed for two weeks.

The ideal muscles of most humans have atrophied.

Every day, jot down ten ideas. Ten company concepts that you can launch. Ten suggestions to improve the business of others. Ten ideas for novels you can write. Ten products that you would make better.

Ten things that upset you in life that you think you can make better. And so forth.

It's nice to have bad ideas. For every excellent idea, you must generate at least 100–1000 terrible ones.

It's said that "ideas are a dime a dozen." Order them to stop talking.

Ideas are a subset of execution ideas. You will be proficient at execution if, after four to six months of idea muscle exercise, you are an idea machine. I promise you this.

4) WRONG PEOPLE

Someone wrote: As you mentioned, I jot down ten ideas every day. I'm overflowing with ideas by the end of the week. I'm giddy with energy and excitement.

Then the speaker went on, "Every Friday night, I go out with my friends, and they all laugh and criticize my ideas."

My response was to stay home on Friday night.

He never got back to me.

You will be depressed by the toxic individuals in your life. Those who are kind to you will cherish and motivate you. It's a pull-pull. Permit the righteous to triumph. Every day, try to make this better.

You can't succeed if negative people keep bringing you down. Your obligations in life are unrelated to this. This is all about preserving your life.

5) IT DRAINS TO BLAME

The following individuals should take the blame: your parents, your instructors, the government, your ex-partner, those who "screwed" you, a terrible broker, and bad this and bad that.

It is your fault. Saying that you are always at fault is exaggerated. I am aware that sometimes horrible things happen that are not your fault.

However, 99.9% of the time, you're probably to blame. That is the simple truth.

I've conducted podcast interviews with hundreds of the world's most prosperous individuals.

Each of them experienced spells of extreme failure. Zero of them said that someone else was to blame for their failure.

The adage "learn from failure" is often overused.

Doing that when you are experiencing the agony of failure is incredibly difficult. I frequently fail at it. Don't blame, though. That is the first step in learning, healing, and going ahead rather than backward.

The moment you shift the responsibility elsewhere, the million-dollar goal gets farther away.

I've gained money, lost money, and made money. Numerous times.

The fact that things fluctuate so much bothers me. I assumed there would be a straight lineup. Am I correct? Perhaps it is for certain people. For Mark Zuckerberg and Larry Page, it appears to have been. I am not them, though. For the most part, I fail. My main desire is an easy existence free from excessive stress. Even while I enjoy working hard on things I love, I don't really want to work too hard.

Something becomes something you enjoy when you start to get good at it. I don't worry about lacking a passion, therefore. Having money is a sign that I'm improving in some areas. And then, either before or definitely after, I begin to adore it.

However, I'm usually taken aback by the emotional roller coaster when it comes to deciding whether or not I deserve the money.

Whatever. I'll take care of it. That's the issue I have. Sincerely, I visit a therapist about it. I have no idea why, but that's how I always feel.

However, I am positive that the other items in this situation are barriers to profit. At least, they have all been my challenges. Perhaps you have other ones.

All of us are human together. We can support one another in overcoming hurdles by sharing our own.

That is the main benefit of being among kind people. That is the essence of being in love. I'm more successful now than I was five years ago because of this. And why, in ten years, I'll be even more prosperous.

Emergencies: The last obstacle to financial success is the unforeseen, which includes illness, death, unemployment, and legal issues. If you don't have an emergency plan, you're at the mercy of random events. Have enough insurance and keep money set aside for emergencies.

Chapter 4

Motivated Money Mindset That Helps

A driven financial perspective that is beneficial

It's natural to feel as though you have little control over finances, at least not in the grand scheme of things. Although you would certainly want a higher wage, you are limited in how much you can bargain for. Or perhaps you reside in a city where there is a significant demand for housing but would prefer a lower rent. When it comes to money, most of us actually feel the complete opposite of being in control—as though our financial decisions are the ones that always determine how we live our daily lives.

However, studies indicate that having a sense of control over your finances is essential. Researchers discovered that people made better financial decisions just by feeling more in control.

Researchers placed some subjects in a room with tall chairs (named the "leaders") and others in a different room with a low ottoman as the only seating choice (called the "followers") in an effort to get study participants in the proper frame of mind. Next, the researchers inquired about the desired amount of savings from both groups. While the followers only saved between 13 and 18 percent of their income, the leaders were willing to set aside between 34 and 42 percent.

No, I'm not saying that your financial problems can be solved by getting a taller chair. However, the authors of the study postulated that people who feel strong want to hold onto that feeling, which motivates them to make choices that will help them feel in control.

With one important exception, a spending plan and a budget are identical: a spending plan supports a cause that is important to you.

"What we need to concentrate on is: What is it in our behavior, and our financial behavior specifically, that we

have the power to change because we cannot control the outside world?"

The following money maneuvers can help you find that power. These are easy steps that will have a significant impact on your mental health and, in the long run, your bank account.

Make Simple Decisions

No matter how much money you save, the act of saving itself can motivate and empower you in unexpected ways. You can't control the job market or the economy, as Clayman points out, so instead of feeling helpless, give yourself the chance to decide on something you can influence. One tiny way you can take some control over your financial situation is to decide to save.

Making decisions that show ourselves we have power over our lives sets us on the path to motivation. The exercise of control is more important than the particular decision we make.

To put it another way, it doesn't matter how much money you save or how much extra you decide to put toward your debt. It's the initial act of decision-making on your part. "This sense of self-determination is what drives us," says the speaker.

Switch to a Spending Plan Instead of a Budget

Diets are difficult because they are meant to be restricting. All you want is a potato chip when you tell yourself you can't have any more of them. Perhaps some french fries as well. Oh, and a milkshake. Sure, please add whipped cream to it.

Budgets pose an identical issue. Most people create a budget because they believe it to be the mature, responsible thing to do. But that resolve to be responsible evaporates when your pals ask whether you want to spend $250 to see Beyoncé perform live.

To overcome this problem, several experts advocate a spending plan instead of a budget. Creating a spending plan involves setting a clear financial objective and creating a budget based on achieving it. Assume for the moment that you want to save $2,000 for a vacation to New York. Your whole financial situation is designed to finance your trip to Momofuku, your Broadway tickets, and all the other things you have planned for your experience in New York City. With one important exception, a spending plan and a budget are identical: a spending plan supports a cause that is important to you.

Saying no to Beyoncé is difficult, but it is much simpler when you have a good reason for doing so. A budget provides you with that rationale. (And I imagine Beyoncé would be happy if it gives you a sense of empowerment.)

Establish a Specific Objective for Your Expenditure Strategy.

"I like to think of working with clients as working on the what and the how at the same time. What is the what, then? Where rubber hits the road, what are you attempting to accomplish? And the how is this: How can we organize the effort we're doing to achieve the goal into a wholesome process?"

Stated differently, determine your initial goals for using your money before attempting to improve your money management skills. It is not necessary for your what to be glitzy. Perhaps all you're seeking to do is get rid of a $10,000 student loan since you can no longer bear the burden. Then, it makes sense to put forth the effort since you are paying to feel free.

Establish SMART Goals

Having a plan makes achieving a goal much simpler as well. The SMART goal criteria provide a simple framework for converting your objective into a plan. It stands for goals that are Time-bound, Relevant, Specific, Measurable, and Achievable. This is an example of a SMART financial goal.

• Particular: I have a $10,000 student loan that I need to pay off.

• Measurable: Using my online student loan account, I will monitor my advancement.

• Achievable: If I reduce my restaurant expenses, I can do this in three years.

• Relevant: Since I want to save money for the things that are important to me, this is relevant.

• Time-bound: I'll pay off this loan by 2021 if I save $277 a month.

And just like that, you have a strategy for achieving the seemingly unachievable task of paying off your student loans. Even so, this at least provides you with a guide to help you cross that finish line.

"I would incorporate markers such as subgoals as well." "Find a meaningful portion of your debt, based on its amount, and treat yourself to a reward or even an effort vacation as you reach those milestones along the way."

For instance, you might give yourself a treat whenever you pay off the first $1,000 of the loan. It doesn't have to be anything ostentatious or lavish because it would be counterproductive. However, you could spoil yourself with something as easy as a lengthy bath, a box of lollipops, or a trip to the neighborhood museum. Recognizing those accomplishments is crucial since it keeps you long-term motivated and process-focused.

Jot down the first memory you have of money.

Money can symbolize a wide range of emotionally charged ideas, depending on the individual: scarcity, wealth, fear, greed, abundance, chance, rage.

"We begin to develop the symbolic quality of money at a young age because we are wired to be emotionally aware of those who raise us.

For example, if money was a frequent source of conflict between your parents, you may have learned to avoid dealing with it because you perceive it as troublesome. You spend thoughtlessly, ignore your budget, and never bother asking for a raise because you'd rather not deal with the chaos. Because our earliest memories of money will always have a significant emotional component, the way we think about money as adults inevitably reflects some of our early experiences with it.

Consider for a moment your earliest financial recollection. Consider the feelings associated with that recollection and how they may have influenced some of your present behaviors. (It could be useful to put it in writing.) You may take a little more control over your financial behavior with this exercise; after all, the first step to changing a habit is realizing it.

Give Up on Automating Everything

Finally, to help you feel more in charge of your finances, interact with them more frequently. Automating every facet of our financial lives is quite simple.

Our bills are automatically paid. To save ourselves from having to type in the digits, we store our credit card information on our preferred websites. However, we frequently don't give those transactions—or our finances in general—much thought, which is the hidden cost of this convenience.

"I think keeping regular contact with our money is the best place to start if most of us are trying to get to a more grounded and financially healthy place." Cut the credit cards off. Review your spending plan each day. Put your spending in writing. Try spending exclusively cash if you're absolutely committed; studies show that consumers spend less when they pay with cash.

It's possible that something that suits one individual won't suit you. Paying with cash may result in you spending more money overall.

Perhaps doing a weekly financial check-in would be more motivating for you than a daily one. While there are certain universally applicable basic financial rules, personal finance is unique. Finding what works for you is the first step to feeling financially empowered.

Chapter 5

Reaching Retirement Financial Independence Techniques for Quickly Building Wealth

Increasing the rate at which wealth accumulates is essential to early retirement planning. People need to be deliberate and proactive when making financial decisions.

Raising savings rates is one way to hasten the generation of wealth. A higher percentage of income saved allows people to build wealth more quickly. This could entail changing one's way of living, including reducing frivolous spending or looking for methods to generate extra cash through side gigs or freelancing.

Cutting down on debt is a further tactic. Paying down high-interest debt allows people to allocate a larger portion of their income toward investments and savings. Their long-term financial objectives may be greatly impacted, and it may even enable them to retire early.

Optimizing returns on investments is also essential for accelerating the building of wealth.

Early retirees need to diversify their investments to reduce risk and increase returns, and they should carefully evaluate how to allocate their assets. To construct a well-rounded portfolio, this may entail investing in a variety of stocks, bonds, real estate, and other assets.

Planning Investments and Allocating Assets for Early Retirees

To guarantee that people have a strong portfolio that produces steady income throughout their retirement years, investment planning is essential. When creating an investing plan, early retirees need to take their time horizon, risk tolerance, and financial objectives into serious consideration.

Asset allocation is a crucial component of early retirees' investment strategy. People can reduce their risk and possibly even boost their rewards by spreading their assets over a variety of asset classes. This could entail making investments in real estate, mutual funds, equities, bonds, and other financial instruments.

The requirement for a well-balanced portfolio is an additional factor.

A combination of income-producing assets, like dividend stocks or real estate, and growth-oriented assets, such as stocks or mutual funds, should be the goal for early retirees. This balance permits capital appreciation in addition to helping to provide a consistent income stream.

Expense management and Budgeting for Early Retirement

Maintaining an early retirement lifestyle requires careful planning and disciplined spending. Early retirees need to prioritize their financial objectives, thoroughly evaluate their spending, and pinpoint areas where savings can be achieved.

Keeping a close eye on your spending is one way to manage a budget in early retirement. People who maintain an extensive log of their expenses are better able to spot areas in which they could be overspending and adjust their spending. By doing this, they can make sure that their retirement funds continue for the full duration of their retirement.

Setting financial goals in order of importance is another factor. Early retirees should budget their resources based on their vital costs, which include housing, healthcare, and daily living expenses. People can make wise decisions regarding discretionary spending and save needless financial stress by concentrating on what is really important.

Handling Tax Consequences and Withdrawal Techniques

To reduce their tax burden and maximize their retirement funds, early retirees must devise tax-efficient exit plans. Utilizing a combination of taxable, tax-deferred, and tax-free accounts helps optimize their tax condition.

To manage tax brackets, one tactic is to take money from various types of accounts systematically. People can benefit from long-term capital gains rates by removing money from taxable accounts, including brokerage accounts. To gradually control their tax liability, they may also think about changing their standard IRAs to Roth IRAs.

Another thing to consider is how Social Security benefits affect taxes. Early retirees should carefully examine when to start claiming Social Security benefits to minimize their tax burden. People who time their Social Security payouts and retirement savings withdrawals may find that their total tax status improves.

The Importance of Passive Income and Side Jobs for Early Retirement

If early retirees develop side enterprises and generate passive income, they can improve their financial independence and security. These businesses, which allow people to follow their passions while providing a steady stream of income, can range from real estate investments to online companies.

Having rental properties is a common strategy to bring in passive income.. By making real estate investments and generating rental income, people can enhance their retirement savings. This could increase their overall value and provide a steady stream of income.

Another option would be to look into freelancing or online companies.

People can now earn money from home in a variety of ways thanks to the digital age. These side ventures, which could include starting an internet business, offering consulting services, or working as a freelance writer, can give early retirees more financial stability and schedule flexibility.

Financial planning for an early retirement is a complicated process that necessitates giving a lot of things significant thought. By employing strategies for accelerated wealth accumulation, maximizing retirement savings through tax-advantaged accounts, optimizing investment planning and asset allocation, implementing effective budgeting and expense management techniques, navigating tax implications and withdrawal strategies, and looking into side gigs and passive income, people can position themselves for a successful early retirement journey.